Mel Bay Presents

SAXOPHONE LICKS, PHRASES & PATTERNS

by Arnie Berle

1 2 3 4 5 6 7 8 9 0

Introduction

Language is any means of expression or communication. There are the spoken languages which make use of vocal sounds. These sounds are combined to form words which make-up the vocabulary used by a particular group of people such as for example, the French, the Italians, the Germans, the English, etc. There is also another language, the language of music which makes use of instrumental sounds to create emotionally satisfying musical compositions. Just as there are different kinds of spoken languages, there are also different kinds of music, for example, classical, folk, rock, jazz etc. Each kind of music also has its own particular vocabulary. The purpose of this book is to study the vocabulary which makes up the language of jazz. In studying any language there are basically two ways you can go about it, the 1st way is to study the alphabet of the language and see how the letters form the words of that language, you then study the grammar and see how sentences are formed by putting words together, and you learn how to read and write in that language. Also you must listen to people who speak that language or at least listen to recordings to hear the inflections and articulations that apply to that language. A 2nd way which is more popular because it is easier and faster, is to get a book which contains the most commonly used words and phrases of that language and through practice and repetition plus listening to recordings of the language you can learn it that way. In this book we are going to study the language of jazz and we will take the 2nd way just described. We are going to study and memorize some of the most commonly used licks, phrases and patterns heard in jazz. Also, you will have to listen to recordings of as many of the great jazz players as you can, listening to how they articulate and inflect as they play. You will have to memorize some of the licks and phrases that you hear first by singing them and then by playing them on your particular instrument. Listen to players on all instruments not just your own. After a while you will come to realize that each of these players has his or her own particular favorite licks and phrases and patterns which can be heard over and over again in an unlimited number of combinations and with many variations. Each player has absorbed in his musical memory bank over a period of time, a whole body of material which can be drawn upon and reconstructed to fit any musical situation. This is true of every great jazz player starting with Louis Armstrong through to Charlie Parker to any of the important players of any era of jazz.

Contents

Licks, Phrases and Patterns

Before we get into the book any further I think we should have an understanding of just what the words Licks, Phrases, and Patterns mean. Sometimes the meanings tend to be fuzzy and overlap according to who is using the words but the following will serve as a good working definition for our purposes.

LICKS

A lick is a short melodic fragment based on a particular chord type such as major, minor or dominant. It is part of a phrase in the same why that a word is part of a sentence. A lick can be as short as two beats or as long as two measures. Sometimes it is called a "run". Below is an example of a lick based on a G7 chord. (Dominant type chord)

PHRASES

A phrase is a connected series of licks which form a complete musical statement. It may be as short as two measures or as long as four measures. It may be part of a longer solo. Below is a phrase based on a frequently used series of chords.

PATTERNS

A pattern is a model to be copied or imitated. A lick or a phrase may be considered a pattern when it is used as model to be played in other keys. In this book we will consider a pattern to be a sequence of notes repeated on different steps of a scale. Below is a pattern based on the C Major scale.

Actually everything in this book may be considered a pattern since in order to get the most benefit from the book you should play all licks, phrases and patterns in ALL KEYS. In the APPENDIX you will see how to transpose all licks and phrases into other keys. This is very important and you should make every effort to understand the principle of transposing.

How to Use This Book

All knowledge is best gained when taken in small doses. Therefore, go through this book slowly. Memorize a few licks of each type, major, minor, and dominant and then move on to the section on phrases. It would be helpful to hear how the various licks sound against their respective chords, for that purpose you should play the chords on the piano in the left hand (voicings are given for the non - pianist in the APPENDIX) and play the licks in the right hand. Guitarists should tape the chords and play the licks over the taped chords. Play everything very slowly to avoid forming poor fingering habits. Play all licks, phrases, and patterns an octave higher or lower wherever possible.

Scale Practice Routine

Although scales by themselves have nothing to do with jazz, the fact is that a lot of jazz licks, phrases and patterns are based directly on scales. The ability to play around every kind of scale is very important in helping you become a good jazz improvisor. The following scale exercises and patterns should be played in every key.

An extended two octave pattern. Memorize and then play in all keys.

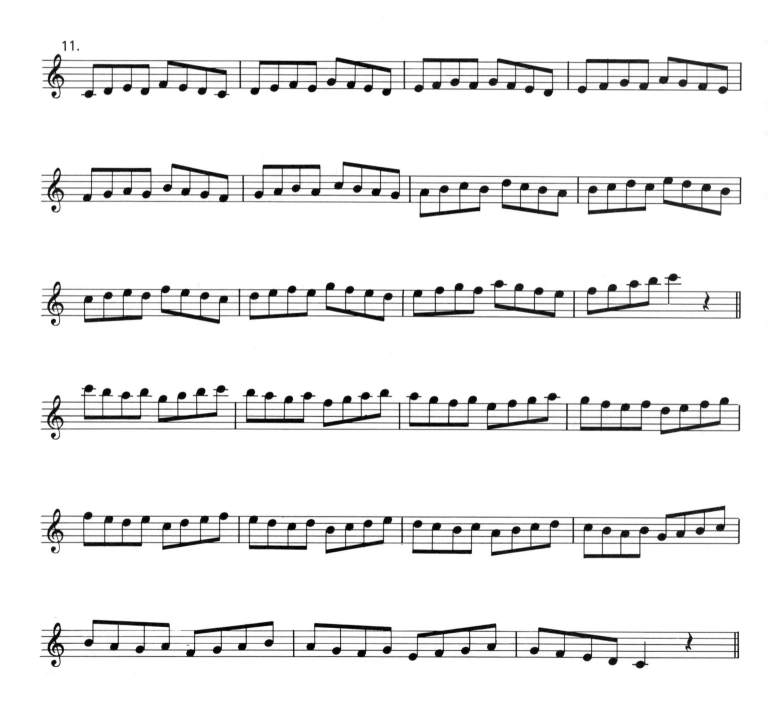

Major Chords-Major Triads

Chords are derived from scales. Below is the C major scale. The numbers beneath each scale note indicate the numerical position of that note within the scale. By extracting the 1st, 3rd, and 5th notes from the scale we form the C major triad. A triad is a three note chord. The symbol for the triad is the letter - name of the triad.

Licks Based on Major Triads

The following licks are based on the C major triad. Since there are only three notes in the triad there are not too many interesting possibilities. You will find that as we add more notes to our chords the licks become more interesting. For now we will begin with these.

Major 6 Chords

The major 6 chord is formed by extracting the 1st, 3rd, 5th, and 6th notes from the major scale.

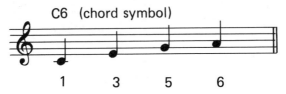

Licks Based on the Major 6 Chords

One measure licks

Two measure licks

Major 7 Chords

By extracting the 1st, 3rd, 5th, and 7th notes from the C Major scale we form the CMajor Seventh chord. Symbol; CMaj7.

Licks Based on Major 7 Chords

When improvising on a Major 7 chord you may also include the 6th of the scale. The following licks will include both the 6th and the 7th of the major scale

One measure licks

Cmaj7

Two measure licks

Cmaj7

Major 9th Chords

By extending the C Major scale to its 2nd octave we can extend our chords beyond the Major 7th. For example, if we extract the 1st, 3rd, 5th, 7th and 9th notes from the two octave Cmajor scale we form the Cmajor ninth chord. The symbol is Cmaj9.

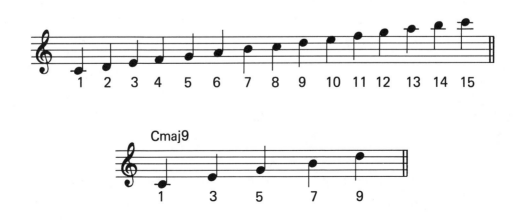

1 2 3 4 5 6 7 8 9 10 11 12 13 14 15

Cmaj9

1   3   5   7   9

Major 9th Licks

The following licks are based on the Major 9th chords. Notice that the Major 7th and the 6th may also be used when the symbol is CMaj9.

One measure licks

Two measure licks

The C Major 11 and C Major 13 Chords

By extracting the 1st, 3rd, 5th, 7th, 9th, and 11th notes from the major scale we form the CMajor 11 chord. A common practice when using the 11th is to raise the 11th a half step. If we add the 13th note to the 11th we form the major 13th chord. Below we see the CMaj11 CMaj9#11, and the CMaj13 chords.

NOTICE: The 11th note is the same letter as the 4th note (F) and the 13th note is the same letter as the 6th (A)

Major Type Licks

All of the following licks are in the key of C and may be played against any Cmajor type chord, CMaj7, CMaj9, CMaj11, CMaj13. When a chord symbol indicates a raised 11 (♯11) then that note, the ♯11 must be included in your lick in order to avoid a clash with the natural 11. Memorize as many of the licks as you can and play them in all the other keys. See the section on transposing in the APPENDIX.

More About Major Type Chords

It is important to remember the following points about all major type chords.

1. The 1st note of all chords is known as the ROOT of the chord. The root is the same as the letter - name of the chord. For example, The root of a CMaj9 chord is C. The letter - name of the CMaj9 is C.

2. Since all of the major type chords that we have learned start from the 1st note of the major scale, we can call all major type chords by the Roman numral I. In other words, all major type chords are known as I chords since they start from the 1st note of the major scale.

3. All major type chords (I chords) are chords of rest and are usually found at the end of a section of music or the end of a progression such as the 11th measure of the blues. Major type chords are also the chords used to establish the key of a piece of music and so they may be found at the beginning of a progression or a section of music. For example, the 1st measure of a blues progression would contain a major type chord. The 1st measure of an 8 measure section such as found in the standard tunes used by jazz players would also contain a major type chord. (there are some exceptions to all rules).

4. When improvising against any major type chord you may use any of the notes in the major scale. Be sure there are no altered notes in the chord symbol such as for example, CMaj7♯ 5. Where there is a raised 11th in the chord symbol then that note must be included in your improvisation. A scale which contains the raised 11th (or the raised 4th which is the same letter) is called the LYDIAN Mode.

* C lydian mode

       1   2   3   ♯4   5   6   7   8

Notice that the Clydian mode is the same as the Cmajor scale with the raised 4th. This is the correct scale to be used for any major type chord which has a raised 11 in the chord symbol such as CMaj9♯11 or CMaj13♯11.

* There is a school of theory that believes that when the major 7th is extended up to the 11th, the 11th is naturally raised. Therefore, since the 11th is the natural extension of the CMaj7 chord it is also more natural to use the Lydian mode when improvising against a major chord. It is not necessary to have that indicated in the chord symbol. The student should experiment using the Lydian mode against the major chord.

Adding Chromatic Notes

so far all of our licks have been madeup entirely of notes within the scale, either the major scale or the Lydian mode, now we are going to add notes that are not in the scale. These notes are the chromatic notes and they help to create a smoother melodic flow. The chromatic notes are those notes which are in between the normal scale tones and generally lead either a half step up or a half step down to a scale tone.

16

17

Dominant 7th Scale-Mixolydian Mode

The Dominant type chords are formed from the Dominant 7th scale. This scale is also known as the Mixolydian mode. To understand how this scale is formed let's look once again at the two octave C Major scale.

Two octave C Major scale.

Our new dominant 7th scale starts from the 5th note of the major scale. In other words, the 5th note of the major scale becomes the 1st note of the dominant 7th scale. Below is a two octave G dominant 7th scale. Note that in order to show a full two octaves I had to start an octave lower.

G dominant 7th scale. (G Mixolydian Mode.)

You should transpose the G Dominant 7th scale to all keys and practice them using the practice routine shown on pages 5 and 6. Remember that the key signature of each dominant 7th scale is the same as that of the major scale from which it is derived.

Dominant Type Chords

By taking certain notes out of the G Dominant 7th scale we form the various G Dominant type chords. You should form the same kinds of chords from the other dominant 7th scales.

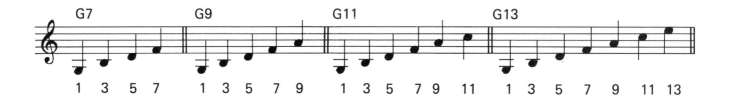

Dominant Type Licks

The following licks may be played over any unaltered G Dominant type chords such as G7, G9, G11 or G13. All licks should be memorized and played in all keys. See APPENDIX for information on transposing.

Dominant Type Licks
With Added Chromatic Notes

The following licks are based on G Dominant type chords and all may be used interchangeably. However, care should be taken when sustaining a chromatic note that is not indicated in the chord symbol. For example, if the chord symbol is G9 do not hold the D♭ which might be in a lick, for a beat or more since it will clash with the natural D in the chord. Transpose as many of the following licks that you like into all other keys.

22

23

24

25

More About Dominant Type Chords

It is important to remember the following points about all dominant type chords.

1. The 1st note of all dominant type chords is called the ROOT of the chord. The root is the same as the letter - name of the chord. For example, the root of a G7 chord is G. G is also the letter - name of the G7 chord.

2. Since all of the dominant type chords that we have learned have been formed starting from the 5th note of the major scale (see page 18) we can call all dominant type chords by the Roman numeral V. In other words, all dominant type chords are known as V chords because they start from the 5th note of the major scale.

3. Anytime you are given the chord symbol G7 you may include the 9th, 11th or 13th (6th) in your solo. If you are given the chord symbol G13 it is not necessary to include all of the notes indicated by the chord symbol in your solo. You can use as few or as many notes as you care to.

4. When improvising against any dominant type chord you may include any of the notes of the Mixplydian mode (see page 18). You may also use chromatic notes if you do not sustain that note for more than an 8th note in order to avoid a clash with the natural note. However, if there are altered notes indicated in the chord symbol such as for example, G7♭5♭9 then it is important that those altered notes be included in your solo. (More about altered chords later in the book).

5. The dominant type chords, the V chords, are chords of movement. They want to be resolved. They create tension unlike the I chords which create a feeling of rest. Dominant chords are generally followed by major type chords although there are many times when there may be a long series of dominant type chords before finally resolving to a major type chord.

Minor 7th Scale-Dorian Mode

The minor 7 type chords are the last of the three important chord types used in jazz. There are a number of different kinds of minor scales which can produce a minor 7th chord however the minor 7th scale we are concerned with right now is the minor 7th scale also known as the Dorian Mode. Below we see how this scale is formed. We start once again with our two octave C Major scale.

Our new scale, the minor 7th scale, also called the Dorian mode, starts on the 2nd note of the major scale. In other words, the 2nd note of the major scale becomes the 1st note of our new Minor 7th scale (Dorian Mode). Below is the full two octave D minor 7th scale.

You should transpose the D Dorian Mode to all keys and practice them using the practice routine shown on pages 5 and 6. Remember that the key signature of the new scale, the Dorian Mode, is the SAME as the major scale from which it is derived. Ex. the key signature of D Dorian Mode is no sharps, no flats, since it is derived from the C major scale.

Minor 7th Type Chords

Again, we take out certain notes from the Dorian Mode to form the different Minor type chords. Notice that there is no minor 13th chord although the 13th (6th) may be used when making up your licks.

Minor Type Licks

The following licks may be played over any unaltered minor type chord. All the licks are based on the
D minor scale or the D Dorian Mode.

Minor Type Licks
With Added Chromatic Notes

The following licks are all based on minor type chords and are all interchangeable. All the licks are derived from the D minor 7th scale or the D Dorian Mode Memorize as many of the licks as you can and then play them in all other keys.

33

Major Type Licks

All of the following licks are in the key of C and may be played against any C major type chord, CMaj7, CMaj9, CMaj11, CMaj13. When a chord symbol indicates a raised 11 (♯11) then that note, the ♯11 must be included in your lick in order to avoid a clash with the natural 11. Memorize as many of the licks as you can and play them in all the other keys. See the section on transposing in the APPENDIX.

Major Chords-Major Triads

Chords are derived from scales. Below is the C major scale. The numbers beneath each scale note indicate the numerical position of that note within the scale. By extracting the 1st, 3rd, and 5th notes from the scale we form the C major triad. A triad is a three note chord. The symbol for the triad is the letter - name of the triad.

Licks Based on Major Triads

The following licks are based on the C major triad. Since there are only three notes in the triad there are not too many interesting possibilities. You will find that as we add more notes to our chords the licks become more interesting. For now we will begin with these.

Major 6 Chords

The major 6 chord is formed by extracting the 1st, 3rd, 5th, and 6th notes from the major scale.

All knowledge is best gained when taken in small doses. Therefore, go through this book slowly. Memorize a few licks of each type, major, minor, and dominant and then move on to the section on phrases. It would be helpful to hear how the various licks sound against their respective chords, for that purpose you should play the chords on the piano in the left hand (voicings are given for the non - pianist in the APPENDIX) and play the licks in the right hand. Guitarists should tape the chords and play the licks over the taped chords. Play everything very slowly to avoid forming poor fingering habits. Play all licks, phrases, and patterns an octave higher or lower wherever possible.

Scale Practice Routine

Although scales by themselves have nothing to do with jazz, the fact is that a lot of jazz licks, phrases and patterns are based directly on scales. The ability to play around every kind of scale is very important in helping you become a good jazz improvisor. The following scale exercises and patterns should be played in every key.

More About Minor Chords

It is important that you remember the following points about the minor chords shown in this section of the book.

1. The 1st note of all minor chords is called the ROOT of the chord. It is also the letter-name of the chord. For example, the root of a Dm7 chord is D. D is also the letter-name of the Dm7 chord.

2. Since all of the minor chords that we have learned have been formed from the 2nd note of the major scale (see page 27) we can call these chords by the Roman numeral II. In other words all the minor chords that we have just studied are known as II chords because they start from the 2nd note of the major scale.

3. When improvising against any II chord you may use any of the notes of the dorian mode from which the chord is derived. Chromatic notes may be used for embellishment but do not hold a chromatic note for more than an eighth note since it will clash with the natural note indicated by the chord symbol. For example, if you are playing a Dm7 chord do not stay on a C$\sharp$ for more than an eighth note and use it only when going to another note within the chord.

4. The II minor chords are used to prepare a dominant type chord. One of the most important series of chords is the II chord going to the V chord. This will be more fully explained in the next section on PROGRESSIONS.

Progressions

A progression is a series of chords which provide the harmony to a given melody. Progressions are also used by jazz musicians as the basis, or the frame, upon which the musician practices the art of improvisation. If one were to examine the large body of tunes used by jazz musicians it would soon become obvious that certain series of chords, or progressions, tend to occur over and over again. Therefore, it becomes important to the aspiring jazz musician to isolate the more common progressions and to learn and memorize as many licks, phrases and patterns based on those progressions, as possible.

Forming the Progressions

Most of the progressions used by jazz musicians are madeup of various combinations of the three different chord types we have just learned. Let's see how these progressions come about. Progressions are derived from scales so we will use the C major scale for our example.

Now we place above the 1st, 2nd and 5th notes of the scale the chords we formed from the modes learned earlier in the book. Over the note C we place the CMaj7 chord which we formed from the C major scale (see page 8). Over the note D we place the Dm7 chord which was formed from the D Dorian Mode (see page 27). Over the note G we place the G7 chord formed from the G Mixolydian Mode (see page 18). Notice that Roman numerals are used to indicate the numbered position of each chord within the scale.

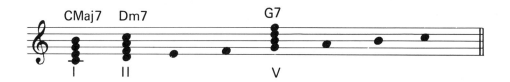

On the following pages we will study the most common progressions found in jazz.

The II-V Progression

The most frequently used progression found in popular as well as jazz tunes is the II-V progression. It is a minor type chord going to a dominant type chord. This progression may be heard in such tunes as Satin Doll, Misty, Confirmation, Cherokee, Bluesette and so many more of the great standards. Sometimes both chords are found in the same measure and sometimes each chord will be played for a measure apiece. Now we will see how the licks we've been playing are combined to create phrases making up the II-V progression. Memorize as many of the following phrases as you can and then learn them in all the other major keys. Eventually you, will be able to create your own licks and phrases.

38

The II-V phrases you've just played had one chord in each measure, a more common use of the II-V progression is to have both chords in the same measure with each chord receiving two counts.

The II-V-I Progression

Another progression found in hundreds upon hundreds of popular and jazz standard tunes is the II-V-I progression. A minor type chord going to a dominant type chord going to a major type chord. A few examples of where this might be found is in the following tunes, MISTY (meas. 2 - 3, 17 - 19), ALL THE THINGS YOU ARE (meas. 17 - 23, 33 - 35), I'LL REMEMBER APRIL (meas. 13 - 15, 17 - 19, 21 - 23, 25 - 27). It would be very beneficial to take some of the II-V phrases you've just learned and try to find appropriate licks(taken from the pages of major type licks that we've had) which would make a complete II-V-I phrase. Use the following examples as your guide.

Here is a phrase based on a II - V progression shown on page 37.

Complete the above phrase by adding on any of the following C Major type licks. This will give you a complete II-V-I phrase.

On the next page will be two more examples of how you can makeup your own II - V - I phrases. You will begin to realize that the more licks you know, the greater your choices when making up your own phrases.

Here is an other phrase based on the II - V progression.

Add any of the following major type licks to the above progression to create a complete II - V - I progression.

Here is one more phrase based on a II - V progression.

Any of the following Cmajor type licks may be added to the above phrase to create a complete II - V - I progression.

45

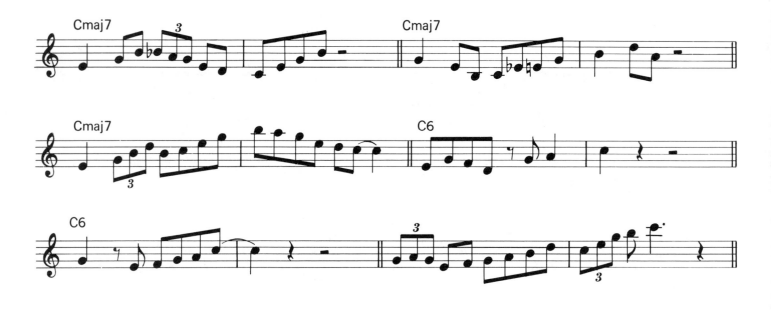

Here now are more II-V-I phrases already worked out for you. All phrases are made up of licks learned earlier in the book.

The I-VI-II-V Progression
(Rhythm Changes)

Another progression is the I-VI-II-V progression. Commonly called "Rhythm changes" since this series of chords were originally found in a tune much favored by the jazz players of the Bebop period of the 1940's, I got rhythm. Notice that there is a chord which has not been discussed yet, the VI chord. The VI chord is built from the 6th note of the major scale. Below is the VI chord shown in the key of C.

Notice also that the notes in the VI chord, Am7, are the same notes as in the I6 chord, C6, Am7 = A-C-E-G, C6 = C-E-G-A. Therefore, in any I-VI-II-V progression you can treat the VI chord as a I6 chord and play any major type licks through the I-VI part of the progression. As a matter of fact, some composers leave out the VI chord altogether and you will see the progression as I-II-V.

Below is an example of a major type lick which could be played over a I-VI part of the I-VI-II-V progression.

Any of the following II-V phrases may be added to the phrase above to complete the I-VI-II-V progression.

When the I chord or the I - VI chords are followed by the II - V chords try to make the licks played for the I chord sound as if they want to move forward. A melodic line should have a sense of direction.

Here is another example of a lick based on a I chord, notice that it sounds as if it wants to move forward.

To complete the I - VI - II - V progression you can add on any of the following II - V phrases.

And still another lick based on a I chord.

Any of the following II - V phrases may be added to the lick above to complete a I - VI - II - V progression.

The Diminished 7th Chord

The diminished 7th chord (the symbol is O7) and its related diminished scale has a number of very interesting applications. Let's first learn how the chord is formed. The diminished 7th chord is built on a series of minor 3rd intervals.

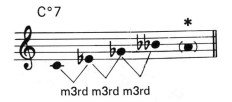

Because the notes of the diminished 7th chord are all equally distant from each other (a m3rd apart) any of the notes in the chord may be considered the letter - name of the chord. Therefore the CO7 chord may also be called the Eb O7, Gb 07, or A07.

* The "A" is the enharmonic equivaler of the double flatted "B"

Diminished 7th Chord Patterns

Play the following C diminished 7th patterns in all keys.

The Diminished Scale

So far all the chords you've learned, except for the diminished 7th chord, has been formed from the notes of a particular scale. The diminished scale on the other hand, is formed by adding notes to the diminished 7th chord. By adding a note a whole step up from each note of the diminished 7th chord we form the diminished scale. Below we see the C diminished scale. The circled notes are the notes of the C07 chord.

The following licks are based on the C diminished scale. Remember that each of these licks may be played over a C07, Eb07, Gb07 or A07 chord.

50

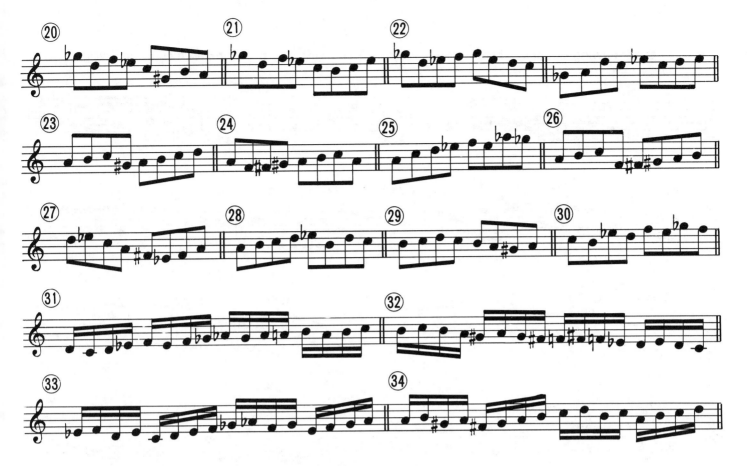

Diminished 7th Chords in Progressions

The diminished 7th chord is often used as a connecting chord between two other chords. For example, it may be used to connect a I chord to a II chord as in the following progression I - I07 - II - V, in the key of C the chords would be CMaj7 - C07 - Dm7 - G7. Another progression would be I - #I07 - II - V, in the key of C the chords would be CMaj7 - C#°7 - Dm7 - G7. The following examples will illustrate the use of some of the diminished licks we've learned in these two progressions.

I-I°7-II-V

In the following examples there are two chords in each measure, therefore, each chord receives two counts.

I-#1°7-II-V

In these next examples the diminished licks are played over a #1°7 chord. You will have to transpose the licks you choose up a half-step since all the licks given are based on C°7.

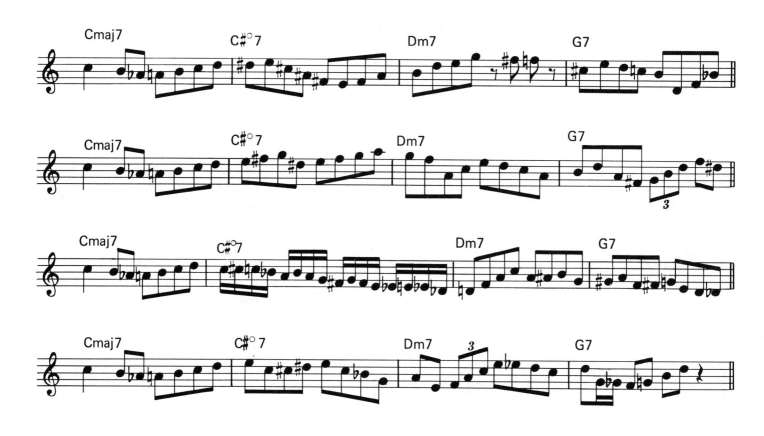

The following examples show the I-#I°7-II-V progression occupying two measures with each chord receiving two counts.

Diminished Licks and Dominant Type Chords

Below is a G7 chord with a♭9th. (G7♭9). Shown also is a B°7 chord.

Notice that by eliminating the root of the G7♭9 chord the remaining notes form the B°7 chord. Therefore, the B°7 may be used as a substitute for the G7♭9. Also, the B diminished scale may be used to improvise over a G7♭9 chord. Since the G7♭9 is just another form of the G7 chord we can also use the B diminished scale over a G7 chord. Using a diminished scale to improvise over a dominant type chord provides many of the colorful notes that makes a jazz solo so exciting to listen to. A simple formula to use which tells you which diminished scale to use for a dominant type chord is to use the diminished scale whose tonic note is a half-step higher than the root of the dominant chord. For example, a G7 chord uses an A♭diminished scale. Remember that each diminished scale has four possible names so the A♭diminished scale is the same as the B diminished scale.

Diminished Scale as Improvising Scale for II-V Progression

Another use of the diminished scale is its use as an improvising scale over a II-V progression. The scale provides some of the interesting and colorful notes that were so typical of the Bebop era. The scale that is used is the diminished scale whose tonic note is the same as the root of the II chord. In a Dm7 - G7 progression use the D diminished scale. The following examples will illustrate the II-V-I progression in the key of C. The D diminished licks are used over the Dm7 - G7 chords. You will have to transpose the licks given in the book since they are all based on a C diminished scale.

More on the Diminished Scale

The diminished scale is one of the most interesting and valuable scales for the jazz improvisor. There are only three different diminished scales, C dim, C♯dim, and Ddim. Each of these three scales has four possible names because of the particular construction of the scales. See below

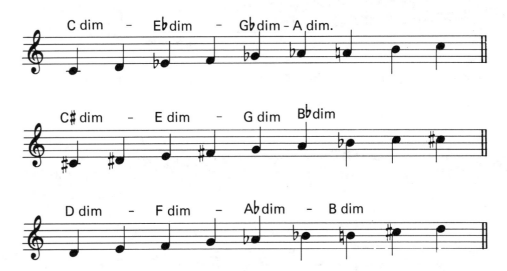

On page 54 we learned that the diminished scale may be used to improvise over a II - V progression by using the scale whose tonic note is the same letter as the root of the II chord. Now we have just seen above that the three basic diminished scales, Cdim, C♯ dim, and Ddim each have three other possible letter - names, therefore, we can say that each of the three basic diminished scales may be used to improvise over four different II - V combinations. The table below lists the three basic diminished scales and the four II - V combinations that each scale may be used to improvise upon.

BASIC DIMINISHED SCALE	II - V PROGRESSIONS			
C dim.	Cm7 - F7,	E♭m7 - A♭7,	F♯m7 - B7,	Am7 - D7
C♯dim.	C♯m7 - F♯7,	Em7 - A7,	Gm7 - C7,	B♭m7 - E♭7
D dim.	Dm7 - G7,	Fm7 - B♭7,	A♭m7 - D♭7,	Bm7 - E7.

Below are examples showing how the same C diminished scale may be used over four different II - V chords resolving to the I chord. In other words, you see how the same diminished lick can be used to resolve to four different I chords.

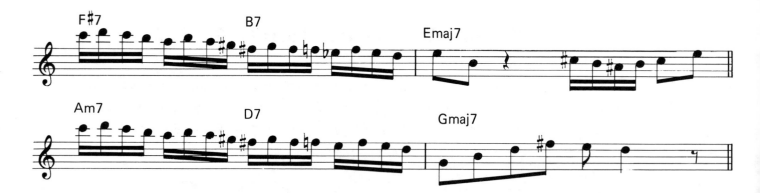

Below we see how a lick based on the C# diminished scale may be used over four different II-V-I progressions.

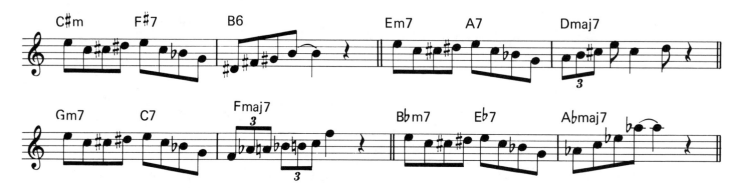

Now we see how the D diminished scale produces a lick that can be played over the last four different II-V chords going to their respective I chords.

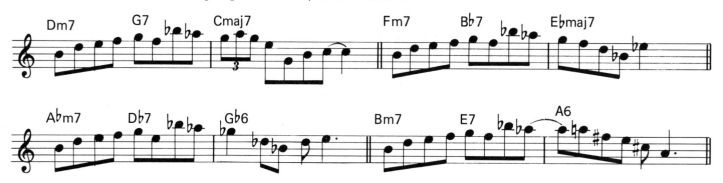

As you can see by the above examples the diminished scale is a very useful scale to be used in a number of different situations. Just three diminished scales can be applied to II-V chords of 12 major keys. The diminished scale may also be used to improvise over just the V chord. To use the diminished scale over a V chord just use the scale whose tonic note is the same letter-name as the 5th of the V chord. For example, over a G7 chord you can use the D diminished scale (D is the 5th of the G7 chord).

Remember: Each diminished scale has four possible names, therefore the D diminished scale is exactly the same as the Ab diminished scale, the F diminished scale and the B diminished scale. Any one of these scales will work well against the G7 chord (since they are all the same scale)

"Rhythm" Changes

Now that you have seen how licks are combined to form two and four bar phrases let's see how we can extend that to the larger eight bar phrase which is more commonly found in jazz. For example, below is an eight bar chord progression which is similar to the first eight bars of the popular tune "I Got Rhythm" written by George Gershwin.

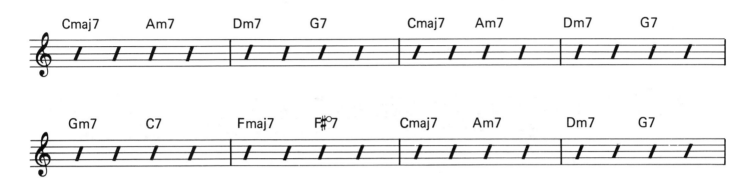

The above progression has been the basis of literally hundreds of tunes used by jazz players· since it was written in the 1930's to the present. You will notice that within the eight bar progression there are three instances of two bar chord progressions that we've already had, the I-VI-II-V is seen in measures 1 - 2, 3 - 4, and 7 - 8. Therefore any of the I-VI-II-V phrases that we've learned can be played in those measures. Here is one possibility.

Since the chord progression is the same in the three places I mentioned meas. 1 - 2, 3 - 4, and 7 - 8, then any phrase that is used in one place may also be used in another place. Below is another possibility.

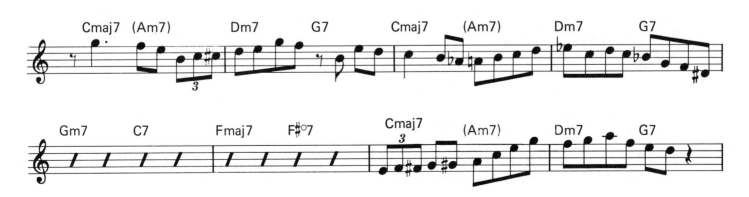

Now to complete our eight bar chord progression we have to play a phrase in measures 5 and 6.
Here are three phrases that will fit those chords.

Any of the above phrases may be used to complete our original eight bar chord progression.
The overriding rule is that good taste should determine how these smaller phrases fit together
to create the larger phrase. Below is the complete eight bar phrase.

Let's continue to use the chord progression known as "Rhythm" Changes as a model for building a longer solo using the licks and phrases we've learned in this book. We've just worked on the 1st eight bars of the tune and now we'll work on the next eight bars. Notice that except for the last two measures, the second eight bars are exactley the same as the first eight bars.

Once again we refer back to our I-VI-II-V phrases that we learned earlier and our II-V phrases and our major and diminished type licks and we come up with the following eight bar phrase.

Now let's look at the chord progression for the next eight bars of "Rhythm" Changes.

You will notice that the above progression is based on a series of dominant type chords, a series of V7 chords. An alternate progression that many jazz players use is shown below. It simply is a series of II-V chords. This follows the rule that any V chord may be preceded by its II chord.

59

Below are two examples of phrases based on the progressions just shown. The first example uses a series of dominant type licks transposed to the correct key. The second example makes use of a series of II - V phrases transposed to the correct keys.

Either of the two examples shown above may be used for the 3rd eight bar chord progression of "Rhythm" Changes shown on the bottom of page 59.

The last eight bar segmant of "Rhythm" Changes is the same as the 2nd eight bar segment shown on page 59. Here once again is an example of what might be played for this last eight bars. Again we have to refer to our I-VI-II-V phrases and our II-V phrases and our major ¹and diminished type licks.

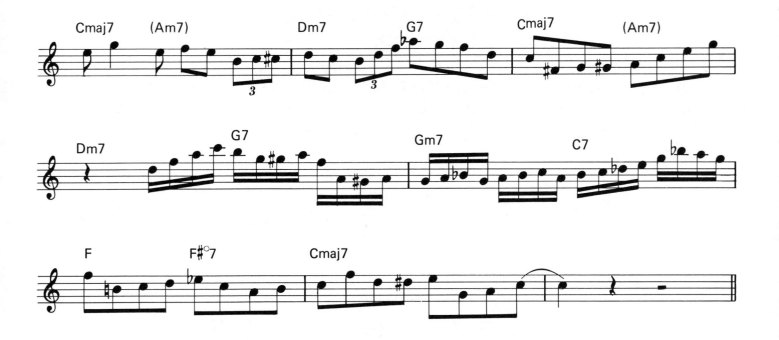

The Standard Song Form

As you've probably noticed the song we've just used to practice our extended phrases is made up of four eight bar segments. Three of those segments are, for all practical purposes, exactly alike. The structure, or form, of the song is known as the American popular song form. It contains 32 bars or, four eight bar segments. Each eight bar segment is given a letter designation so as to identify that particular eight bar segment. For example, the first eight bars is called letter. "A" Since the next eight bar segment is the same as the first eight bars we can call that segment letter "A" also. The third eight bar segment is very different from the first two eight bar segments so that we give it the letter "B". The last eight bar segment is the same as the first eight bars so again we can call that letter "A". The structure is now identified as the AABA form. This 32 bar AABA form is, next to the 12 bar blues form, the most popular form for musical, compositions used by jazz musicians. Thousands of the great standard tunes of 1930's and 1940's employ this 32 bar AABA form. It would be good for the student to search out these great standard tunes and practice creating your jazz solos in the same manner as we just did on pages 57 through 61.

The Blues Progression

The most important musical form in all jazz is the 12 bar blues. From the very beginnings of jazz through all the various styles of jazz the blues has been the favorite vehicle for the improvising musician. Below is a very basic blues progression.

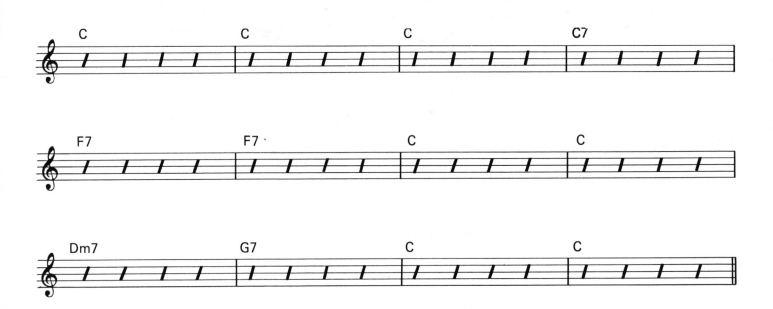

One of the commonly used devices of the blues is to play a dominant type lick over a major type chord. The dominant type lick supplies what is called the "blue" notes which are so characteristic of the blues. We will learn much more about the blue notes in a little while. Below is an example of an improvisation based on the blues progression. All licks and phrases are taken from those learned earlier in the book.

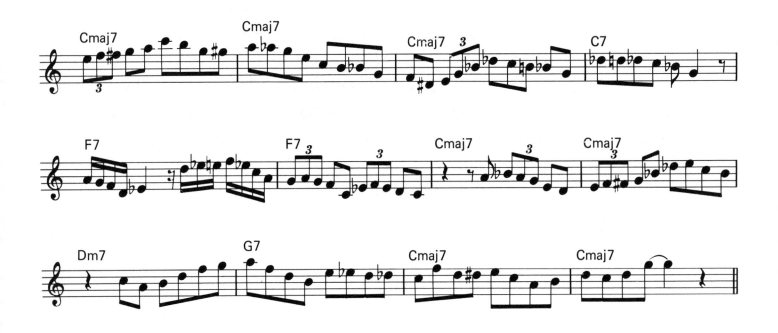

Another more modern blues progression is shown below. Notice the frequent use of the II-V chords. Notice also the I-VI-II-V progression in the 7th, 8th, 9th and 10th measures.

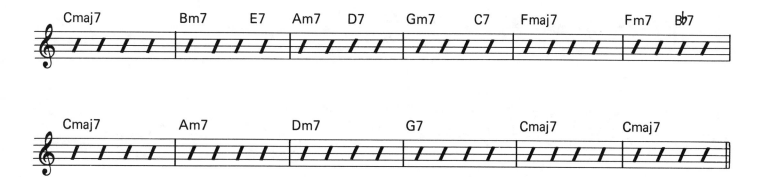

Below is an example of a solo based on the above chord changes. All licks and phrases are taken from those we learned earlier in the book

Below is another prossible improvistion based on the blues progression.Notice that in the 5th measure the chord is now an F7 chord rather than an FMaj7 chord. Also notice the II-V chords in the 12th measure. This is known as a "TURNAROUND". A turnaround is a sequence of chords that turns you around or, turns you back to the 1st measure of a section of music. When playing the blues it is most common to play more than one chorus, so rather than end on a I chord which brings the progression to a close, the II-V chords are used to bring you back to the I chord in the 1st measure of the progression. When playing the last chorus of blues you can end on the I chord.

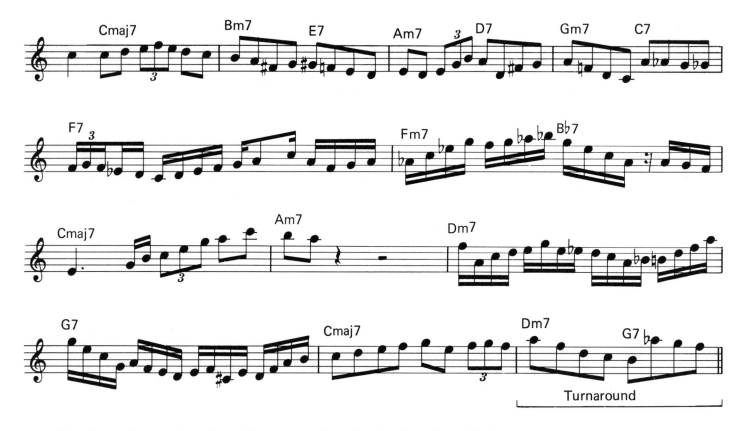

Here is another version of the blues progression. Notice that all Cmaj7 chords are now played as dominant 7th chords. This is very common in the blues

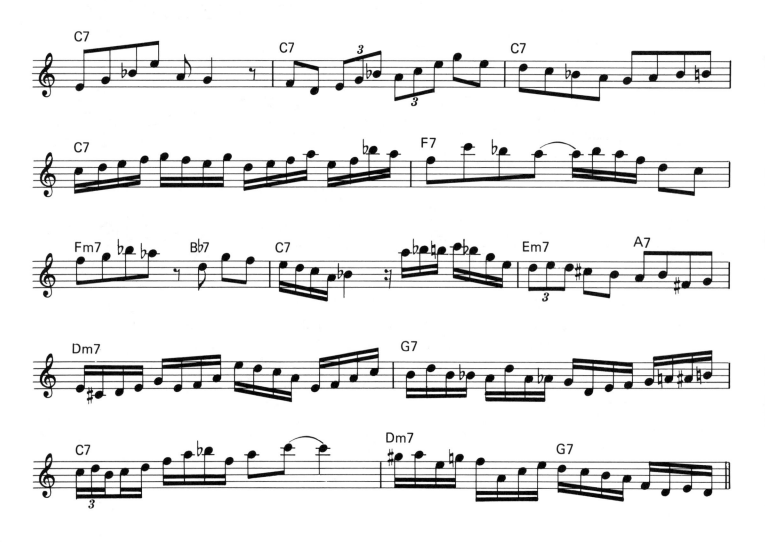

Blue Notes-Blues Scale

From the time that the blues was first heard back in the early 1920's certain notes seemed to be heard over and over again. These notes could be heard in the singing of the blues singers and in the playing of the musicians. These notes were such a characteristic part of the blues that they were called the "blue notes". These blue notes are simply the ♭3rd, ♭5, and ♭7th notes of the major scale. Eventually these blue notes evolved into the "blues scale". Below are the blue notes in the key of C and the C blues scale.

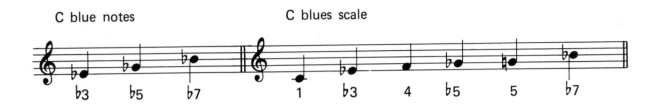

Notice that the formula for the blues scale is the 1st, ♭3rd, 4th, ♭5th, 5th and ♭7th notes of the major scale.

Blues Licks

Below are some licks based for the most part on the notes of the C blues scale. If you include too many notes that are not in the blues scale you tend to lessen the blues quality of your solo.

The following blues solo is based entirely on the C blues scale. This scale is excellent for beginning the study of improvisation since the whole scale can be used for the entire progression of the blues.

Here is one more example of a blues chorus madeup entirely of the one blues scale. Remember to use the blues scale of the key you are playing in. The following blues is in the key of C and utilizes the C blues scale. You will note that occasionally notes belonging to the indicated chord may be used but the blues scale is still the predominant sound.

The blues scale may also be used to improvise over a dominant 7th chord and a minor 7th chord. Many jazz players use blue notes in their solos and the blue notes have become characteristic of jazz in general and not confined to only the blues forms.

Here are some examples of the blues sound incorporated into G7 chords resolving to the I chord.

Analyzing Licks

It should be obvious at this point that you cannot expect to be a jazz player by just playing other people's licks. It's now time to learn how to make up your own licks. But in order to do that we should take a more analytical look at some of the licks you've already played and try to come to some understanding of just what makes up a lick. Below is a lick that we had earlier in the book, it's a dominant type lick based on a G7 chord.

Some of the points of interest are listed below.

1. The use of sixteenth notes to create the feeling that the piece in which this lick is taken from as being played at a faster tempo than it really is. This is called playing with a "double time feeling". The tempo is slow but you're playing more notes per beat which gives the effect of the tempo being played twice as fast.

2. The 1st note of each group of 4 sixteenth notes is a chord tone. The note A in the 2nd group of sixteenth notes indicates that the chord is a G9 rather than a G7.

3. The notes played on the downbeats are all chord tones.

4. The 1st 3 notes in the 1st 2 groups of sixteenth notes are arpeggiated chord tones. Also the 1st 2 notes in the 3rd group of sixteenth notes is chordal.

5. The last 7 notes of the lick are played scale - like. The lick is a good balance of chordal and scalar playing.

6. Chromatic notes B♭, A♭ and A♯ are used to connect chord tones in a smooth flowing manner.

7. The 1st 2 sixteenth note groupings are known as a sequence, that is, a little melodic figure that is repeated on another note of the scale. This helps to create melodic interest.

8. The melodic flow is well balanced. The 1st 2 sixteenth groupings descend and the next 2 sixteenth note groupings ascend.

Here is another lick for analysis. It is another dominant type lick

POINTS OF INTEREST

1. Note the rhythmic variety. You have a quarter note, sixteenth notes, eighth notes, and a triplet.

2. The one count A on the 1st beat establishes that the chord is a G9th. The chromatic notes B♭ and G♯ are lower neighboring tones to the chord tones. They provide a little tension which quickly disappears when followed by the chord tones.

3. The last 3 sixteenth notes are arpeggiated chord tones and the triplet is a scale - like figure.

4. The shape of the melody is interesting since it begins on a high note, instantly dropping to a lower note and works its way up again only to head back down with the triplet.

Here is still another lick based on a major type chord.

POINTS OF INTEREST

1. The last 4 eighth notes in the 1st measure outline a C6 chord.

2. Major type chords are used to complete a phrase or to provide a sense of having arrived. A release of tension. This lick does all that.

3. The F and D♯ on the 2nd beat are not chord tones but they are the upper and lower neighbor tones of the note E which follows. They kind of set up a bit of tension only to be released by playing the E.

4. Notice that it is not necessary to fill every beat of every measure with notes.

Here is a II - V phrase that we can analyze for its interesting points.

POINTS OF INTEREST

1. Notice the interesting rhythmic variety starting with the syncopated figure for the first two counts. The quarter note in the 2nd measure which breaks up the long flow of sixteenth notes giving the listener a chance to reflect on what he's just heard. The sixteenth rest before starting off again on another run of sixteenth notes.

2. The E on the 3rd beat 1st measure indicates a Dm9th chord. The C♯ and the E in that same grouping of sixteenth notes act as upper and lower neighbor to the D which comes on the 3rd beat.

3. The use of chord tones is very pronounced in the 1st measure but is balanced off by the more scale - like notes on the 1st and 3rd beats of the 2nd measure. The 4th beat is a return to the arpeggiated notes of the G7 chord.

4. The notes G and E on the 1st beat of the 2nd measure act as upper and lower neighbors to the F on the 2nd beat.

5. The quarter note F in the 2nd measure and the last note B in the same measure are the important notes of the G7 chord(7th and 3rd are the two most important notes in a dominant type chord). These two notes create the tension that is characteristic of the dominant type chords. You can hear them leading you into the Major type chord which usually follows the dominant type chord.

Here is another II-V phrase in the key of C.

POINTS OF INTEREST

1. The eighth rest on the 1st beat shows that you don't have to start playing right on the 1st beat.

2. The C♯ is the lower neighbor leading into the triplet which begins on the D, the root of the chord. A very common figure.

3. The note C on the 3rd beat with the G7 Chord is the upper neighbor to the chord tone B.

4. The A♭ in the G7 chord although might be considered the b9th of the G7 chord, appears in this situation to be acting as a chromatic passing tone down to another note (G) which would normally follow as part of the C major type chord which usually follows a G7 chord.

Conclusions

Before beginning to makeup your own licks and phrases you should analyze more of the licks and phrases that we've had in this book as well as others you might have aquired on your own. Below is a listing of some of the obvious factors that should be considered in playing any improvised solo. The following list could also be used as a guide as to what to practice in preparation for making up your own licks and phrases or any improvised solo.

1. Since our analysis of licks and phrases showed that there is a good use of both chord and scale tones it becomes very important that anyone wishing to improvise have a thorough command of both chord arpeggios and scales. Therefore a regimen of practice should include the arpeggiating of all kind of major type chords, dominant type chords and minor type chords plus an intense study of the scales which each of the chord types come from such as the major scale for major type chords, dominant 7th scale for dominant type chords and the minor 7th scale for minor type chords. Patterns such as those given on pages 5 and 6 should be applied to all the scales just mentioned. Additional patterns for both chords and scales are given on pages 72, 73, and 74.

2. In our analysis we learned that oftentimes chord tones seemed to follow notes that seemed unrelated to the chord being played. These "unrelated chord notes" were the upper and lower neighbor notes which surround each chord note. There are many ways of using these neighboring tones. The student should work out some of these many combinations. Examples will be given on pages 75 and 76.

3. Continue to listen to records and add to your repetoire of licks and phrases. Learn how to vary a lick by changing the rhythms around. There are many books available which contain transcribed solos of the great jazz players, learn these solos and analyze them for those sounds that most appeal to you and incorporate some of those ideas into your own playing.

Patterns for Improvising Technique

Now that you've acquired some of the vocabulary of jazz by playing and memorizing a variety of jazz licks and phrases and you have also learned how to analyze what makesup a jazz lick there is one further factor we must consider before you are ready to makeup your own licks and phrases. You must develop some jazz technique on your instrument. When you are given a series of chords or a chord progression to improvise on it's too late to try to figure out what the notes are in each chord as indicated by the chord symbol. It's too late to try to figure out what scale is indicated by the chord symbol. All of the knowledge must be thoroughly ingrained in your mind and your fingers have to be trained to react instantaneously. The only thing that you should be concerned with is the content of the solo. Although this kind of practice takes years of concentrated effort I would like to offer some studies that will help in this kind of jazz technique development.

CHORD ARPEGGIOS AND SCALES

Below are several exercises based on the different chord types that we've had combined with their related scales. All exercises are based on the key of C but as you will see I have indicated the order of keys in which each exercise should be practiced.

EX. ①

Notice that in the following patterns the 1st note of every 4 note groupings is a note of the chord.

Each of the above patterns should be played in the following order of keys.

1. C - F - Bb- Eb-Ab- Db- Gb- B - E - A - D - G   2. C - Eb- Gb- A.   3. Db- E - G - Bb.   4. D - F - Ab- B

5. C - Db- D - Eb- E - F - Gb- G - Ab- A - Bb- B -   6. C - D - E - Gb- Ab- Bb.   7. Db- Eb- F - G - A - B.

The following patterns are all based on the Dm13 chord and the D minor 7th scale.

Each of the above minor chord - scale patterns should be played in the same order as listed for the major chord - scale patterns. For example, Cm13, Fm13, B♭m13 etc.

Continue through the same sequence of keys. Remember that the minor 7th scale is the same as the dorian mode. Be sure to play with the correct key signature. For example, the key signature of the Cm13 patterns is two flats (B♭ and E♭)

The following patterns are based on the G13 chord and the G dominant 7th scale

Again, play each of the above dominant chord - scale patterns in the same order as listed for the major chord - scale patterns. For example, C13, F13, B♭13, E♭13 continuing through the rest of the sequence of keys. Remember that the dominant scale is also known as the mixolydian mode and you should be sure to know the correct key signature for each pattern.

Making Up Your Own Licks

At this point, having gone through the material in this book, you should be making up your own licks and phrases. If you are still having trouble with that then perhaps the following will help.

When beginning to improvise it's always best to start with the smallest fragment of a solo and that is the lick. Also, it's best to start with just the notes of a chord and keeping the rhythm very simple. Below is a lick based on a CMaj7th chord. We will see how this lick develops through several stages and you can use this as a model for your own licks.

A simple arpeggiated form of the CMaj7 chord with the added 6th (A). The 6th is often used with the Maj7th.

A rhythmical variation on the original lick.

Another rhythmical variation. Illustrates that you don't have to play on every beat.

Placing scale tones between the chord tones gives a more scale - like effect.

Another scale - like lick with a little variation on the 3rd and 4th beats.

The use of sixteenth notes produces a double - time feeling. When a piece is played at a slow tempo this creates a greater interest.

⑦

Lick No.7 is another lick which gives a double - time feel. Notice the use of the neighboring tones in the first three groupings of sixteenth notes.

In the above examples you were able to see the development of a simple lick to one more complex and modern sounding. Let's try a lick based on a II-V progression. The following lick is based on Dm7 - G7.

①

Just a reminder that licks don't have to start on the root of the chord.

②

A simple rhythmical change can make a big difference.

③

A more scale-like approach does away with the exercise sound of too many arpeggiated notes.

④

Another way of disguising the arpeggiated notes

⑤

A slight change in the melodic shape creates more interest.

⑥

Another rhythmical variation

⑦

Introduces more chromatic notes. Another rhythmic variation and a double - time feel.

⑧

Note the use of neighboring tones on the 2nd and 3rd beats.

Improvising on Altered Chords

All of the various licks and phrases in this book may be used against unaltered chords. Licks and phrases that contain chromatic notes not indicated by the chord symbols (G7 ♭5 ♭9) will not clash with the chords because the chromatic notes are being used as embellishing tones and are followed by either a chord tone or a scale tone. Also you have been told a few times that a chormatic tone should not be sustained unless that note is indicated in the chord symbol otherwise there will be a clash with the natural note. Now there are many times when you will be given chord symbols that do have altered notes in them such as G7♭5, G7♯5, G7♭9, G7 ♯9, G7♭5 ♯9, etc. In such cases it is very important that those altered notes be included in your improvisation other wise by using the unaltered note you will produce a clash. Below are some of the possible altered chords.

Major 7$^{\sharp 11}$ – Major 7$^{\flat 5}$

The major 7th chord with the ♯11th (sometimes written as ♭5) will use the lydian scale. Note that the word scale is being used in place of mode. All modes are scales

Major 7$^{\sharp 5}$

The major 7th ♯5 uses a Lydian - Augmented scale. Although this scale also includes the ♯11, it is not necessary in the chord symbol. As a matter of fact there is a whole school of theory that believes the ♯11 should be included in all improvised solos against any Major type chord even without the ♯11 in the chord symbol.

Dominant 7♭5 or♯11

When a dominant chord has a ♯11th in the chord symbol the correct scale to use is the Lydian - Dominant scale. This scale should also be used with a dominant 7th chord with a ♭5th. The scale below is the G Lydian - Dominant scale, notice that it is our old dominant 7 scale (mixolydian mode) with a raised 4th. This scale is also referred to as the G Lydian ♭7 scale.

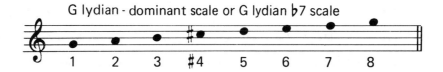

G lydian - dominant scale or G lydian ♭7 scale

Dominant 7♯5

A dominant 7th chord with a ♯5 uses a Whole - tone scale. Notice that this scale also contains a ♯11th. The scale may also be used with a dominant 7♭5 chord although the preferred scale is the Lydian - Dominant.

G whole tone scale

Dominant 7♭9

A dominant 7th chord with a ♭9 uses an altered dominant scale. An altered dominant scale is a dominant scale which contains one or more of the four possible altered notes to be found in chord symbols. The following altered dominant scale contains the ♭9 (shown as a ♭2).

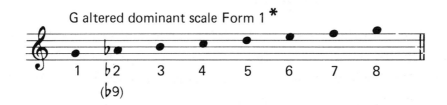

G altered dominant scale Form 1 *

* For the purposes of identification we can call this scale Form 1 altered dominant scale.

Dominant 7 ♯5 ♭9

A dominant 7th chord with a ♯5 and ♭9 uses the following altered dominant scale. We will call this a Form 2 Altered Dominant scale.

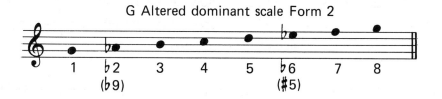

G Altered dominant scale Form 2

1 ♭2 3 4 5 ♭6 7 8
(♭9)   (♯5)

Dominant 7 ♯5 ♭9 ♯9

A dominant 7th chord with a ♯5, ♭9, ♯9 uses the following altered dominant scale. We will call this a Form 3 Altered dominant scale.

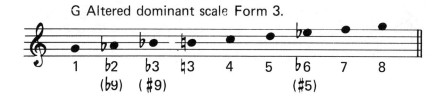

G Altered dominant scale Form 3.

1 ♭2 ♭3 ♮3 4 5 ♭6 7 8
(♭9) (♯9)   (♯5)

Dominant 7 ♯5 ♯9 ♭5 ♭9

A dominant 7th chord with a ♯5, ♭5, ♭9, ♯9 uses the following altered dominant scale. We will call this a Form 4 Altered dominant scale. This scale contains all of the four possible altered notes.

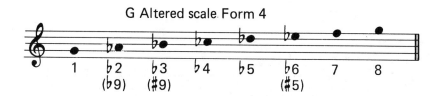

G Altered scale Form 4

1 ♭2 ♭3 ♭4 ♭5 ♭6 7 8
(♭9) (♯9)   (♯5)

An important point to remember is that when given any chord symbol which indicates altered notes just use the scale which you would normally use and include those notes which are indicated in the chord symbol. If there are notes in the scale which might conflict with the chord tones do not stress those notes but use them as passing tones to other chord or scale tones. Try making up your own licks on the scales you've just learned.

Appendix
How to Transpose

In order to get the maximum benefit from the material in this book it is important that you learn all licks, phrases and patterns in all keys. To do this you must know how to transpose from one key to another key. This presupposes that you already know the notes and the key signatures of all 12 major keys. If you don't know all your major scales then you should start learning them now. If you know all your scales then the following technique will help you in transposing the licks into other keys of your choice.

Below is an example of one of the licks shown in the section on major type licks. Notice that beneath each note there is a number which tells you the numbered position of each note in the lick in relation to the root of the chord. For example, the R refers to the root of the chord, the 3 refers to the 3rd of the chord, the 5th refers to the 5th of the chord, the 9 refers to the 9th, the ♯11 refers to the ♯11th of the chord and so on throughout every possible note in the chord.

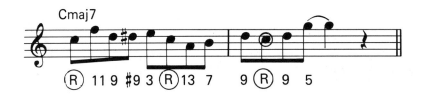

By applying the same numbers to the root of the major chord in any key you can transpose the above lick to any key that you want. Here are three examples.

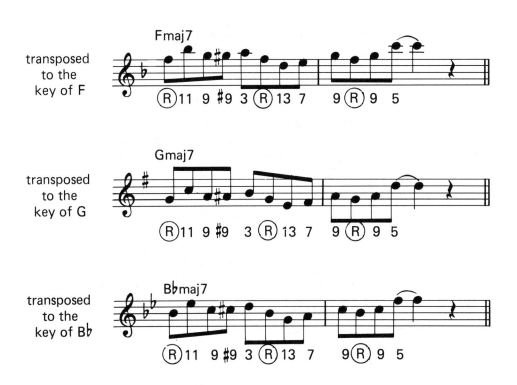

Here is an example of a dominant type lick which we want to play in other keys.

Here is the same lick applied to several other keys.

Here is an example of a minor type lick which we might want to play in other keys.

Here is the same lick transposed to three other keys.

To transpose a diminished lick it would be best to write out the diminished scale from which the lick is taken and place a number beneath each note in the scale and then write out the diminished scale that you want to transpose to with similar numbers and use the numbers in the same way as you did above. Here is an example of a diminished lick we want to transpose to other keys.

In order to transpose the lick based on the C°7 chord let's first write out the C diminished scale and place numbers beneath each scale tone.

C diminished scale

Assuming that you want to transpose the diminished lick to a F diminished lick let's write out the F diminished scale and place numbers beneath each scale tone.

F diminished scale

Now looking back on our diminished lick we transpose the numbered scale tones to the new key.

Let's transpose our diminished lick to an A diminished lick. Write out the A diminished scale with the numbers beneath each scale tone. Although we learned earlier that the C diminished scale is the same as the A diminished scale, when we write out the A diminished scale with A as the 1st note, the numbered position of each scale tone changes.

A diminished scale

Here's our original C diminished lick transposed to A diminished.

NOTICE: Great care must be taken to write the correct number beneath each scale tone. You can devise any method you like as long as you remain consistant.

82

Keyboard Accompaniment
for Non-Keyboardists

Any musician who wants to be able to improvise, and is not a keyboardist, should be able to sit at a piano and play the licks and phrases given in this book as well as those licks or phrases he has madeup on his own, and play the chord accompaniments in the left hand. This is a very excellent way of developing ones ear and preparing yourself to hear the different chord types that you will come across in a real "live" improvising situation.

Below you will find a chord voicing for each of the different chord types that we had and some basic accompaniments for the various progressions we have had. All chords are written in the treble clef for those non - bass clef readers, but, it must be remembered that although written in treble clef all chords are played with the left hand and played in the area of the key board just below middle C.

MAJOR TYPE CHORDS

The following chords are given in all keys and should be played to accompany all major type licks played in all keys.

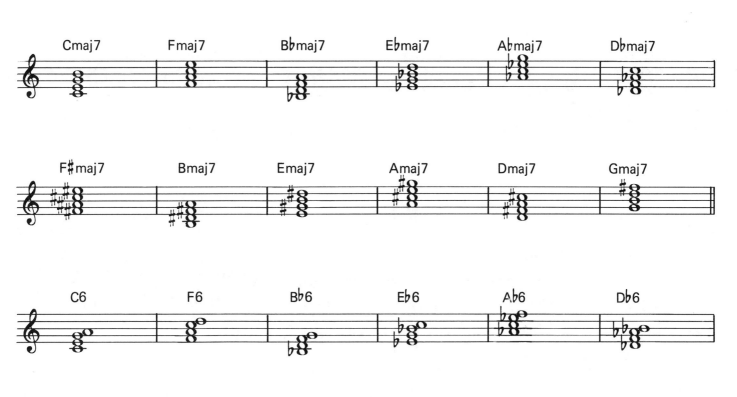

DOMINANT TYPE CHORDS

The following chords are to be used to accompany all the dominant type licks.

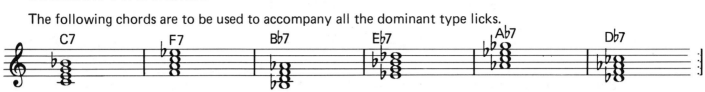

MINOR TYPE CHORDS

The following chords are to be used to accompany all the minor type licks.

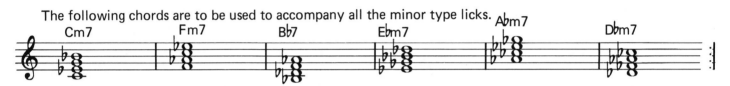

DIMINISHED TYPE CHORDS

The following chords are to be used to accompany all the diminished type licks.

II–V Progression

The following chord voicings may be used to accompany the II-V progressions. Notice that the voicing for the V chord is different than what you just played for the dominant type licks. You can use that voicing if you prefer; however, the voicing given below creates a smoother movement from the II chord.

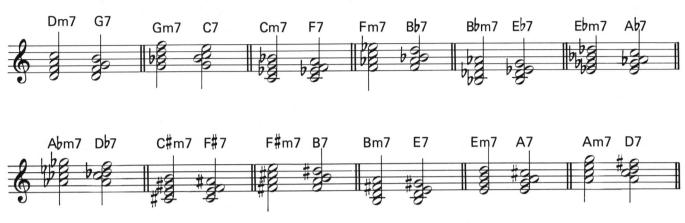

II–V–I Progression

To accompany the II-V-I progression you can use the same chord voicings as shown above for the II and the V chord and for the I chord you can play the voicings used for the major type chords shown on page 83. Below is an example in the key of C.

I–VI–II–V Progression

The following chord voicings may be used for the I-VI-II-V progression. You must understand that there are many ways of voicing these chords. The examples I have given are basic and will allow you to hear the chord type well as you play the phrases in the right hand.

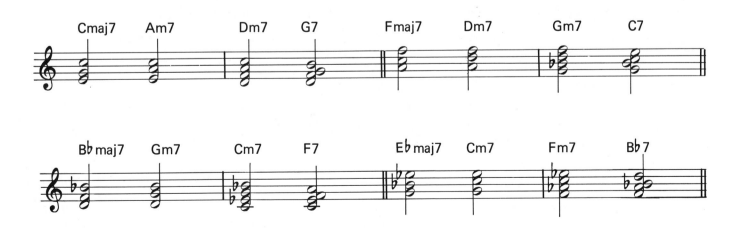

I-I°7-II-V Progression

For this progression it is best to play the I and I°7 chords with the root tones as the lowest notes followed by the II - V chords played as we've been doing in the above progressions. Below is an example in the key of C

I-#I°7-II-V Progression

In this progression it is also best to play the I and #I°7 chords with the roots as the lowest notes and the II and V chords as we've been doing in all the above progressions. Here is an example in the key of C.

Great Music at Your Fingertips